INTRODUCING YOUR DOG TO THE NEW BABY

Written By: Sam Hall

INTRODUCING DOG TO BABY

There's one member of your family that may have some objections to your impending arrival: your canine companion. Unfortunately, there's no way to directly tell poochie that things are about to change in your home in a big way. But, you can do several things to ease the transition for everyone involved.

BEFORE BABY COMES

Preparing your pup for the big changes ahead should start as soon as possible. While you may need to spend lots of time preparing for baby, you need to be sure not to neglect your puppy-mom duties. Much like an older sibling to be, pups can become quite jealous about time they don't get from their parents.

Taking your pooch on lots of pregnancy walks and spending extra time with him will benefit you as well. You'll get additional exercise from all that walking (a highly recommended regimen for expectant mothers anyway), and you'll have the opportunity to reinforce any commands your pup has learned in your tutelage.

If you haven't spent much time on training, now is a good time to teach your pup all of the basic commands you will need to have at the ready when baby comes along. Sit, Stay, and Lie Down are the essentials, but you may want to go further than that depending on your pup's aptitude and your own time constraints.

A great command that your dog should know is something to get them to BACK OFF when necessary. Eventually, your baby will be crawling on the floor, and must be able to do so unmolested. You'll likely have a few last-minute diaper changes on the floor, and play sessions where doggie will need to maintain his distance.

Choose your command first. Some examples are Away, Git, Go Lay Down, and Back off. It needs to be something you won't say in the course of your everyday interactions with Fido. Grab a handful of treats, and practice saying your command with an accompanying gesture, then tossing the treat a few feet away and praising your pooch when they go get it. Eventually, you'll move to only presenting the treat when they've moved far enough away. Graduates of "Git" will eventually back off a few feet without any food rewards, but this may take a while.

Another great command for your pooch to learn prior to baby's debut is "Touch" or "Gentle." You want to be able to allow your pup to investigate the new arrival without fear that he will be too rough right away. Choose your command, and give your pup treats when they simply touch you with their nose, rather than an all-out lickfest they may wish to bestow. When baby comes, you'll be able to communicate to your pup that they may "Touch" or "Gentle" the baby, but not slather the munchkin in doggy drool.

Don't be surprised if doggy regresses in his training slightly when baby actually comes along. You'll want to come up with a plan to help him through it, but the bottom line is it's an exciting time for everyone, pooch included, and that means it will be easy to forget his manners.

When it comes to shifts in the overall lay of the land in your home, you'll want to prepare pooch as much as possible. If he won't be allowed in the baby room, or if his bed and food and water dishes will be moved to make room for baby, do this months ahead of time. This way, the baby doesn't represent a huge shift in his environment, and he can focus on building a relationship with the newbie.

Think about any expectations you'll have for your dog, and put them into practice now. Will he not be allowed on the furniture anymore? Will he have to sleep on the floor now that you're planning on co-sleeping. Set up the crib or bassinette and train puppy to leave them alone now, so it's about the furniture and not about the baby.

Some dogs are extremely possessive of their belongings, such as their food dishes, bed, and certain toys. If you think this might apply to your dog, move their items to an area that will be easily shut away from the baby (try the laundry room or a bathroom where you can easily close the door). It will take years before your little human will understand that there are things to be left alone, so remove the temptation and the danger.

If you can, prepare your dog for contact with children as much as possible. Enlist your mom friends to bring kiddos by for a play date with doggie, and monitor the situation closely. Little people do all sorts of weird things that grown-ups just don't. They move suddenly, get up in doggie's face, and make loud, unexpected noises. All of these things are difficult for some dogs to get used to.

If you're really unsure about your pup's reaction to kiddos, try simply going on walks with a neighbor that has a kid, and gradually bring Rover nearer to the stroller as you walk. This will associate one of his favorite activities with being around a kiddo, and give him the skills and confidence he'll need when baby joins you for your constitutionals.

If your dog is super successful in child interactions, encourage your neighbor children to pet, play, and interact with the pup as much as possible. You may even choose to re-route your walks by a local park or playground to give Fido plenty of experience with little people. By the time your new arrival makes his way onto the scene, your dog may be old hat at dealing with little children.

Get your puppy used to sharing the attention at home as well. If your instinct tells you this may be a difficult transition for doggy, consider purchasing a doll and lavishing attention on it periodically, asking your dog to treat the doll as you would expect him to treat the baby.

Taking your stroller along for your doggy's walks will allow him to get used to walking next to the stroller with you in control. This may seem simple, but it's actually a monumental feat of coordination for both of you. Watch out for stray paws!

A baby comes with a myriad of new smells that are really strange. Allow your dog to sniff new items such as baby powder and diaper wipes. You may not be able to prepare them for dirty diapers, but then again there's no preparation for that.

If your doggy has any other bad habits, it's time to address them right now. You'll have plenty on your plate keeping baby happy and healthy without training your pooch to stay out of the trash or not jump up on guests. Consider enrolling him in doggy day care or obedience school, so he can learn what he'll need to know to get along in your growing household.

PLAN FOR LABOR

You'll want your pooch to be comfortable and not alarmed when the big day arrives and you head off to the hospital. Consider your options for caring for Fido, and choose one way ahead of time. Keep in mind that you may be gone for several days depending on labor length and recovery, so choosing an option that's flexible is essential for a stress-free time for all involved.

If you choose to board your pup, choose a boarding home that he or she is familiar with. Barring that, make sure to take your pup by (if allowed) for a few hours beforehand so that they can get used to the sights and smells of the new place. Remember, you want baby's arrival to be as stress-free as possible for everyone. Be sure that your boarding facility is well-informed of the situation beforehand, and inquire as to the flexibility regarding length of stay and date of arrival.

A more appealing option may be to have a trusted friend (who is familiar with your pooch) stay with them or look into them from time to time. This way, even though he will most certainly know something's up, he'll be in his own home environment. Again, make sure to choose someone willing to be available at a moment's notice, as babies can have a mind of their own when it comes to arrival dates.

Having puppy stay at home will also make the arrival with baby easier, as pooch will hopefully be settled at home and not recovering from some "traumatic" experience at doggy day care.

THE ARRIVAL

When you're bringing your child home to meet the puppy for the first time, you'll want to take several steps to ensure that the meeting is successful. With dogs, as with people, first impressions are very important!

Allow other members of your party (like dear daddy) to walk into the house first, and give your canine friend plenty of love and attention. Wait a few minutes for the initial greetings to take place, so that there is less likelihood of a mishap right at the door. You don't want put yourself in the position of scolding your dog right away when baby first enters the house!

Have a helper leash your dog as you bring in the baby, to avoid any jumping or lunging when he realizes there's something very interesting and new in your arms. Praise and pet him with the baby in your arms, and try to allow the "Touch" or "Gentle" command to do its work. If your pup hasn't mastered this with your hand yet, continue training sessions until they do.

When you enter the house, maintain a positive and upbeat attitude as much as possible. Likely your dog is already quite nervous from all of the excitement in the house, and they will pick up on your own emotions. If you're unsure how your pup will behave around your baby, he will be unsure of how to behave.

Encourage people present for the arrival to split their attention between baby and dog. After all, not everyone can hold the baby at the same time, and it will be good to get your tiny human used to sleeping in the bassinette or crib for naptime as much as possible anyway. Don't let doggy feel ignored right away.

Keep interactions between the pup and your baby brief and very closely monitored. Praise your dog every time he successfully interacts with your child, and distract him with plenty of attention at every opportunity.

If your dog becomes fearful or cowers during the introduction to baby, don't force him to interact right away. Allow the introductions to happen gradually, and work hard over the next few days to help puppy become used to baby. This is where your "Touch" or "Gentle" command can also come in handy. Be sure to use lots of praise every time your fearful canine interacts with your baby positively!

THE FIRST FEW DAYS

The entree of your squalling babe onto the scene is going to inevitably be a point of curiosity for your canine companion, and you should encourage him to investigate under strict supervision. Continue to praise and pet your dog often when the baby is present.

At the same time, you'll want to reinforce this positive behavior around baby by mainly having fun with your pooch when baby's around. Try ignoring your pooch during naptimes (in fact, this is the time you should be catching some zzz's anyhow), and praising, petting, and playing while baby is awake. This will reinforce that baby is a source of fun and excitement.

Whenever possible, avoid speaking harshly to puppy during these first few days. Instead, use treats and distractions to give your commands more weight, as you did during training sessions. It may be a good idea to purchase some toys and treats specifically for when baby is around, to make things extra fun.

Encourage puppy to stick around during feedings if he's curious, but at a safe distance. You may want to move the dog bed close to where you'll be, and let him enjoy your crooning and singing to baby as well. To keep him calm try tossing a bone or a chew toy down next to you at the beginning of the feeding. This should keep them entertained and out of the way for the moment.

Make sure that you do your best to maintain your dog's routine as best you can during this time. Missed feedings and walks are sure to breed a bit of resentment, regardless of the amount of new and exciting happening inside your home. Enlist the help of friends and neighbors if necessary to allow you to focus on baby, or to let you step out for a few minutes with your cute canine.

IF YOUR PUP SHOWS AGGRESSION

An aggressive dog may be acting out for a number of reasons, and the most humane thing to do is to try and change the motivations your dog has for acting aggressively. Start out slowly, playign with the dog while the baby is nearby, so that he gets used to enjoying himself around baby.

Be sure to remove any likelihood that pup's possessions are being tampered with, and consider the location. Are his things in a place where he will be able to enjoy them? Does he have a safe place to retreat into quiet when necessary? Make sure to provide for these factors as best you can.

You'll want to enlist professional help as soon as possible if your dog consistently displays aggression toward your little one. Be sure to choose someone that has a history of working with dogs with aggression issues. A discount trainer may be tempting, but an inexperienced hand can make things worse in these situations. Talk to their previous clients and find out where their skills truly lie.

Keep baby and aggressive dogs separate and safe. Don't leave your child alone with your dog for an instant during this transition period no matter the circumstances, but especially if puppy displays aggression. It takes less than a second for things to go horribly awry.

If there is no successful conclusion to aggressive behavior, you'll want to work on re-homing your pooch. This can be heartbreaking for all involved, yet living in a home with a child is simply more than some puppies can handle. Be sure to investigate any new home thoroughly, and communicate clearly about the issues going on.

You won't want to resort to a shelter unless absolutely necessary, as the chances of aggressive dogs finding homes from a shelter are slim to none. If you absolutely can't take it anymore, or you feel that your baby might get hurt, enlist the help of a foster or animal rescue in your area. Every good dog deserves a home, and just because your dog doesn't enjoy your kiddo's company doesn't mean they are a hopeless cause. Let them bring joy to another home without children to stress them out.

Thank You!

We hope you enjoyed the book! All pictures and words were lovingly put together by experts who really love what they do! We really hope you learned something new today!

We would really appreciate it, if you could PLEASE take the time to let us know how we're doing by leaving a review on the Amazon website. We appreciate any comments you may have – what you enjoyed about the book, what additions you would have liked to have seen and what you would like to see in future publications.

Any comments will help understand better what you and your kids most enjoy and allows us to better provide exactly what you want!

Thought Junction Publishing

A NOTE FROM THE WRITER

Sam's life revolves around her family, devoted mother of 3 - Noah (6), Oscar (3) and Poppy (11months) - she writes in a real way, aiming to answer the questions that other books don't cover, to fill in the blanks and inform parents and parents-to-be of the truth about raising children in the modern world.

Sam's writings emphasize that the readers are not alone - that there is a community of support available, and other people to talk to who can help, support and assist.

When she's not writing books, Sam is an advisor and avid blogger for Ideal Parent - http://ideal-parent.com - spreading support, care and advice across the web!

Join Sam on Ideal Parent and keep an eye out for her books - she's on a mission to help parents worldwide - join her and spread the word!